Privacy Impact Assessment
for the

Immigration and Customs Enforcement Child Exploitation Tracking System (ICE-CETS)

January 19, 2010

Abstract

The U.S. Immigration and Customs Enforcement Child Exploitation Tracking System (ICE-CETS) is a centralized information repository that assists law enforcement in conducting child exploitation investigations. The ICE-CETS database allows information about related investigations to be shared and tied together to reduce redundant investigative work. ICE has conducted this Privacy Impact Assessment (PIA) because personal identifiable information (PII) is maintained in ICE-CETS.

Overview

ICE-CETS is owned and managed by the Child Exploitation Section within the ICE Office of Investigations, Cyber Crimes Center. The ICE-CETS database contains investigative information related to Internet-facilitated child sexual exploitation crimes, to include but not limited to the possession, distribution and manufacturing of child exploitation images and videos (i.e., child pornography) and child sex tourism. The primary purpose of the system is to consolidate tips related to these crimes into a single database; to track, link, and disambiguate the tips; and to prioritize and refer them to ICE agents for investigation. ICE-CETS is not a case management system for these investigations, but is a repository and tool that facilitates the efficient use of investigative resources by ensuring related tips are identified and assigned for proper follow up.

ICE-CETS stores tips related to Internet-facilitated child sexual exploitation crimes, such as a website containing child sexual exploitation material. These tips usually consist of Internet-related data that is somehow connected to the crime, which law enforcement may be able use to identify persons involved in the criminal activity and/or to connect related crimes. An example would be a list of Internet Protocol (IP) addresses from a server that contained images of child exploitation. Currently ICE receives thousands of tips from international and domestic law enforcement sources and non-governmental organizations (NGOs). Examples of such sources include ICE domestic and foreign field offices, the public (through the DHS public tip line), local law enforcement agencies, foreign law enforcement agencies, INTERPOL, and NGOs involved in preventing and detecting child sexual exploitation.

ICE receives both individual tips and tips in bulk. Most tips arrive by email or other secure means including digital media (such as hard disks, flash drives, CDs, or DVDs). Tips from the public are usually delivered by individual emails or phone calls, and can contain a variety of information about whatever suspected crime is reported. Tips from law enforcement and NGOs may also contain Internet data (IP addresses, email addresses, web site addresses (URL)[1], online identifications (IDs), server logs, file logs, voice mail summaries and other identifying data). ICE-CETS does not store any identifying information about victims of these crimes. The system may contain comments entered by CES personnel during tip input pertaining to a suspect, such as age range of the victims a suspect is targeting or the number of images of child exploitation the suspect may have downloaded.

---

[1] A Universal Resource Locator (URL) is a web address like "http://www.ice.gov."

Received tips are entered or uploaded, depending on volume, into ICE-CETS. Authorized personnel in the Child Exploitation Section[2] (CES personnel) review them to determine if they are actionable (i.e., whether they contain plausible information that can be verified through investigatory means and that, if verified, may constitute illegal conduct). Non-actionable tips are marked as such in ICE-CETS and no further action is taken on them. Actionable tips go through an intake process that allows CES personnel to link tips that may pertain to the same offender.

The intake process for actionable tips uses tools in ICE-CETS to compare them with other tips in the database and identify those that might be related based on a common data point, such as an online ID, email address, IP address, an online resource such as a URL, or a suspect's name. If related tips are identified by the system, ICE-CETS notifies the user who then decides whether the tips are actually related and, if so, links the tips in the system. By identifying related tips, new information about a suspected offender is revealed that may be helpful in building a case against that offender. For example, identifying related tips in ICE-CETS may reveal that a single offender using the same IP address is using multiple online IDs to possess and distribute images of child exploitation. Related tips are referred to the same ICE field office for investigation, thereby avoiding duplicative investigative work and ensuring the investigating ICE Special Agent has all relevant information to pursue the case.

Once tips are merged or de-conflicted, CES personnel then prioritize them based on the severity of child endangerment. CES personnel prioritize and pursue the tips based on available investigative resources.

Once prioritized, CES personnel research the tips to enhance the initial information received using standard investigative techniques such as administrative summonses or subpoenas[3] and searches of government, public, and commercial data sources. While the investigative research is not performed in ICE-CETS itself, the results of such research are noted in the system. In cases where subpoenas are issued, typically they are served on entities such as Internet Service Providers (ISPs) and corporations that may have records pertaining to online access and use. ICE issues subpoenas by email, fax, or mail to the relevant entity.

ICE generally only subpoenas the following information as permitted by 18 U.S.C. § 2703: name, address, records of session times and durations, length of service (including start date) and types of service utilized, subscriber number or identity, including any temporarily assigned network address, and the means and source of payment for such service (including any credit card or bank account number). No other information is requested. Information received in response to a subpoena is entered into ICE-CETS. If the subpoena returns useful information, CES personnel refer the tip to an ICE field office for investigation using a DHS system known as TECS.[4] The CES personnel manually enter any relevant data from ICE-CETS into TECS, where the ICE field office to which the matter is referred accesses and assigns it to an ICE Special Agent for investigation.

---

[2] ICE-CETS is used by ICE Special Agents, Criminal Research Specialists, and Criminal Research Officers.
[3] ICE Special Agents have several administrative summonses and subpoenas (hereinafter "subpoenas") at their disposal which may be used in furtherance of these investigations. See Question 1.6 for more information.
[4] The referrals entered into TECS and any subsequent ICE investigative files that are opened are part of the DHS/ICE-009 External Investigations System of Records, 73 FR 75452, Dec. 11, 2008.

Due to the sensitivity of the information contained within ICE-CETS, direct access to the system is limited to CES personnel. Information in ICE-CETS may be shared outside of ICE on an as needed basis with other law enforcement agencies with which ICE is coordinating investigations in accordance with the governing law and policy. ICE also discloses very limited information from ICE-CETS to entities on which an administrative subpoena is served in order to request relevant records pertaining to the tip.

Typical Transaction

A foreign law enforcement agency conducts an investigation and seizes IP addresses from a server containing images of child exploitation. The agency emails a file containing the IP addresses and case background information to the ICE Cyber Crimes Center because the IP addresses are associated with computers that are located within the United States. CES personnel then format the file for ICE-CETS intake and upload the data into ICE-CETS. ICE-CETS software processes the data and creates a new record for each tip (i.e., one record for every IP address). As each new record is created, the system searches existing records for a match. If a new record matches an existing record (i.e., IP addresses are the same), ICE-CETS alerts the CES personnel and allows them the option to link the new record with the existing record. The CES personnel then use publicly available IP lookup services to identify the entity believed to own the IP address in question. Once the entity has been identified, CES personnel serve an administrative subpoena on the entity seeking information about the subscriber of the IP address on the particular date and time in question.

Once a response is received from the entity, CES personnel review the information provided and enter it into ICE-CETS. If the information received in response to the subpoena is actionable, CES personnel send an investigative referral using TECS to the appropriate ICE field office along with a digital copy of the subpoena and response. The field office may request additional information from the Child Exploitation Section related to the investigative referral. If the subpoenaed information deemed not actionable, no investigative referral will be generated. In some cases, the entity's response may indicate that a different entity owns the records requested, in which case CES personnel will issue an additional subpoena to the newly identified entity. In some cases, the entity may no longer have the relevant records. In all cases, the tip will be maintained in ICE-CETS for future reference and it will be updated to reflect the results of the subpoena.

Section 1.0 Characterization of the Information

The following questions are intended to define the scope of the information requested and/or collected as well as reasons for its collection as part of the program, system, rule, or technology being developed.

1.1 What information is collected, used, disseminated, or maintained in the system?

ICE-CETS stores information on individuals that are the subjects of tips concerning the possession, distribution and/or manufacturing child exploitation images and videos, or concerning other child exploitation violations such as child sex tourism. ICE-CETS collects tip information (such as an online IDs, ISP, URL, domain name, hosting company[5], IP address, and the relevant date, time, and location information associated with suspected criminal activity) and biographical information about a potential suspect (such as their name, date of birth, place of birth, and gender if available). Tips may also contain information that was seized from server transactions, or were supplied by other law enforcement agencies such as: motor vehicle information (vehicle type, make, model, license plate), Social Security Number, and credit card number and transactional information. The tips received by ICE do not usually contain the name of the suspected offender, but ICE will place that information in the database if it is included in the tip.

ICE-CETS also contains information gathered via the research process from other government, public, or commercial databases. For example, ICE-CETS may contain the suspected offender's address, which was obtained from public sources or from a commercial data aggregator. ICE-CETS also contains information gathered through the subpoena process, usually from an entity such as an ISP or corporation. The information obtained under subpoena typically includes information about the subscriber of the Internet service (name, subscriber number, billing address, IP address, method of payment, and associated email addresses), a log of the subscriber's online activity, downloads and uploads for the date/time specified in the subpoena, a list of the subscriber's online identities, and any profile information voluntarily populated by the subscriber. Data received through the subpoena, such as the subscriber's name, online identities, and any other relevant information is entered into ICE-CETS to allow further analysis and merging of related tips. If a tip results in a referral to the field for investigation or pertains to an existing investigation, the official TECS case number is entered into ICE-CETS for reference purposes and to ensure that any related tips identified in the future are referred to the same field office for follow up.

ICE-CETS can also generate statistical reports based on information that is stored within its database. Statistical reports will typically contain information such as a tally on the number of tips (in the form of IP addresses, for example) received during a month, the number of subpoenas issued during a month, or the number of cases opened as a result of ICE-CETS referrals to the field.

1.2   What are the sources of the information in the system?

Tips are received from ICE field offices and attaché offices; INTERPOL, EUROPOL, and other international law enforcement agencies; the Virtual Global Taskforce (VGT); foreign law enforcement agencies; state and local law enforcement agencies; NGOs involved in preventing and detecting child sexual exploitation; and members of the public who contact ICE. Law enforcement agencies may receive information through evidence seized during a criminal investigation or from other sources such as suspects, witnesses, informants, and members of the public.

ICE obtains information from various government, public, and commercial databases that it queries in the normal course of its research into tips to determine if they are actionable by the field. In addition to the Internet, the databases routinely queried by CES personnel during the research process are:

---

[5] Hosting (also known as *Web site hosting*, *Web hosting*, and *Webhosting*) is the business of housing, serving, and maintaining files for one or more Web sites.

TECS, the National Crime Information Center, and commercially available databases. ICE obtains information about which entity is the owner of a particular IP address from online, publicly available IP lookup services. ICE also collects information about individuals who are suspected of participating in illegal activities identified in tips from ISPs and other entities that are served with subpoenas.

Finally, the system itself is the source of statistical reports on the number of tips entered, subpoenas sent, and cases referred.

1.3 Why is the information being collected, used, disseminated, or maintained?

ICE collects this information to support the efficient and effective analysis and investigation of tips regarding crimes related to child exploitation. ICE-CETS improves ICE's efforts to detect and prosecute these crimes by assisting in linking tips that may pertain to the same offender and deconflicting targeting among ICE's investigating offices. Information collected through the research and subpoena process is collected to determine if a tip contains valid information, and to gather additional information pertaining to the tip that may allow the tip to be investigated by ICE field agents. ICE-CETS also facilitates the efficient generation of subpoenas by providing a central repository of tips that document the information that leads to the subpoena. Finally, ICE-CETS is also used to generate statistical reports to determine the effectiveness of ICE-CETS.

1.4 How is the information collected?

Law enforcement agencies around the world lawfully seize potential evidence during investigations and receive information related to child exploitation from suspects, witnesses, informants, and members of the public. The tips that are sent to ICE may come from seized server logs, hard drives, data (such as logs) provided by entities, the URLs of sites hosting potentially illegal material, or other information gathered during the course of an investigation or law enforcement activities. Tips may also be collected through telephone calls, emails or voicemails from concerned citizens communicated to law enforcement agencies or NGOs.

ICE receives tips from other law enforcement agencies and organizations in the form of digital media (such as hard disks or flash drives, CDs or DVDs) or through secure email communication. ICE also receives tips from NGOs via secure email communication. Tips are sent to ICE using various mechanisms depending on their format. For example, media may be hand-delivered, or sent by a secure courier. Tips received from the public may be sent to ICE via email.

CES personnel conduct research by directly querying government, public and commercial databases, and inputting relevant results into the CES record pertaining to the tip. Information returned to ICE in response to a subpoena typically is sent by fax and/or email, and relevant information will be entered into ICE-CETS manually by CES personnel.

1.5 How will the information be checked for accuracy?

The accuracy of the tips received by ICE will be checked by CES personnel by conducting research into the tip, including issuing a subpoena for records from the appropriate entity, where appropriate. For example, if a tip indicates a particular IP address is involved in a criminal activity on a particular date and time, the entity may have activity logs that will indicate who was utilizing the service at that time. In some cases, the subpoena does not return any additional relevant information, and consequently the tip will not be referred to the ICE field office for investigation. Any discrepancy between tip information already in ICE-CETS and ICE's research or information received via the subpoena process will be noted in ICE-CETS by the CES personnel who receive and review the response to the subpoena.

The information received in response to an ICE subpoena is usually considered accurate because it is part of the subpoenaed entity's business records and knowingly supplying false information in response to a subpoena constitutes false statements, which is a federal crime under 18 U.S.C. § 1001. If an individual is ultimately prosecuted as a result of the ICE investigation, the reliability of subpoenaed sources can also be challenged in court where the defendant has the opportunity to contest the accuracy and appropriateness of evidence.

Once an ICE field office receives a referral from the Child Exploitation Section, it will determine if an investigation into the alleged criminal activity is warranted. It is the field office's responsibility to verify the veracity of the supplied information through standard investigative methods. If the field office discovers that information in a referral is inaccurate, the field office will notify the Child Exploitation Section, which will update and/or remove the inaccurate record from ICE-CETS after a review by the ICE-CETS Program Manager.

In cases involving IP addresses, ICE uses publicly available IP lookup services to identify the appropriate entity for subpoena service. Due to the complexity of IP architectures, the identification of an entity based on an IP address alone is not always possible because entities may lease IP address blocks to other entities and such arrangements may not be reflected in the IP lookup service databases. If ICE subpoenas an entity that does not own the IP address in question, the entity will not have the records ICE seeks and will inform ICE that it does not support the IP address in question. In such cases, CES personnel will conduct additional research to identify the appropriate entity resulting in additional subpoena service. In the case of leased IP addresses, the original entity will inform ICE to whom it has leased the IP address and ICE will then issue a subpoena to the new entity.

1.6 What specific legal authorities, arrangements, and/or agreements defined the collection of information?

The Electronic Communications Privacy Act of 1986 (Pub. L. 99-508 § 201, codified at 18 U.S.C. § 2703) authorizes the release of certain basic subscriber information upon service of an authorized administrative subpoena by a government entity. The Tariff Act of 1930, chapter 4, subtitle III, part III, Sec. 1509 (19 U.S.C. § 1509) allows for collection of this type of information by Customs Summons when there is probable cause to believe an importation into the United States has been made.

Crimes involving exploitation of children often involve international distribution; as a result investigations of these crimes are part of ICE's enforcement mission. *See* 6 U.S.C. § 203; 19 U.S.C. §§ 482, 1305, 1461, 1467, 1469, 1499, 1509, 1583, and 1589a; DHS Delegation No. 7030.2, "Delegation of Authority to the Assistant Secretary for U.S. Immigration and Customs Enforcement" (Nov. 13, 2004). These images are collected as part of ICE's role in assisting in federal, state, local, and international detection and prosecution of crimes falling under 18 U.S.C. § 2251 et seq. Additionally ICE formalized its arrangement with National Center for Missing and Exploited Children in a Memorandum of Understanding on June 22, 2004 to aid in the collection of child exploitation tips for law enforcement purposes.

1.7 <u>Privacy Impact Analysis</u>: Given the amount and type of data collected, discuss the privacy risks identified and how they were mitigated.

Privacy Risk: ICE-CETS may store tips that contain inaccurate information about individuals, which may lead to an investigation of those individuals.

Mitigation: Law enforcement personnel are trained to critically analyze and independently verify tips they receive that indicate potential criminal activity before acting on such information. Protections provided by the U.S. Constitution, federal law, federal rules of procedure and evidence, and agency investigative policies and procedures all seek to ensure that inaccurate information is identified during the criminal investigatory process to ensure the rights of the accused. In the context of ICE-CETS, the investigatory process for any tips deemed actionable (including the subpoena process) is likely to uncover inaccurate information in the tip which will be considered by the investigator in determining if there is sufficient cause to continue the investigation. Furthermore, field office investigations are responsible to verify the veracity of the supplied information through standard investigative methods.

Privacy Risk: ICE-CETS may incorrectly identify tips as related when in fact they are not.

Mitigation: Users of the system must decide whether tips identified by ICE-CETS are actually related or not, based on the users' judgment, training and experience in law enforcement. Tips that appear to be related are not automatically merged by the system. This mitigates the risk that technology will determine which tips are in fact related, and reduces the risk that unrelated tips will be linked in the system. In cases where it has been verified that a linked tip is not valid, the link may be deleted by the system administrator, or the tip information may be updated to remove any links it previously had.

Section 2.0 Uses of the Information

The following questions are intended to delineate clearly the use of information and the accuracy of the data being used.

2.1   Describe all the uses of information.

ICE receives tips pertaining to child exploitation from various law enforcement and non-profit sources throughout the world. CES personnel input tips into ICE-CETS for the following purposes:

1) Tracking and organizing tips received;

2) Automatically flagging tips that may pertain to the same offender (based commonalities in online identity, email address, IP address, URL, suspect name) so that CES personnel can decide if the tips pertain to the same case and link the records;

3) Analyzing the tips to determine whether they fall under the jurisdiction of other law enforcement agencies;

4) Facilitating research and subpoena generation to verify and expand the information in tips, to record the results of research and subpoenas, and to determine whether tips are actionable;

5) Referring actionable tips to the appropriate ICE field office or other law enforcement organizations for further investigation; and

6) Generating statistics on the performance and effectiveness of ICE-CETS.

In cases where any physical evidence, through chain of custody, is received in conjunction with a tip, whether this is in the form of hard copy or digital media, the fact that such evidence was received will be documented in ICE-CETS by authorized CES personnel and the evidence will be stored in accordance with ICE's standard evidence procedures. This evidence will be sent to investigating ICE field offices when requested. Physical evidence is not stored in ICE-CETS and at no time will a digital copy be made of the evidence for the purpose storing it in ICE-CETS.

2.2   What types of tools are used to analyze data and what type of data may be produced?

During the intake process, ICE-CETS automatically checks to see if any existing tips pertain to the same offender as the new tip (based on commonalities such as online identity, email address, IP address, online resource such as a URL, suspect last name, or suspect given name) and flags the match for CES personnel. The CES personnel determine whether the records appear to pertain to the same offender and, if so, link the tips. Any linkages to an existing tip that was previously referred to the field for investigation will cause a notification to be sent to the assigned CES personnel for that tip. The assigned CES personnel will then send the updated information to the ICE Special Agent or field office assigned to the investigation of the original lead so they are aware that new information related to the case has been received.

Notifications of ICE-CETS users occur inside the ICE-CETS system itself using in-system messaging. ICE-CETS sends an in-system message to a user's account with information detailing new links to one or more of their assigned tips. Users can also send messages to one and other while logged into ICE-CETS.

ICE-CETS can also generate reporting statistics on the number of records, cases, subpoenas, and referrals produced for management purposes.

2.3   If the system uses commercial or publicly available data please explain why and how it is used.

CES personnel perform direct queries of commercial databases and publicly available data in the course of conducting research on tips in ICE-CETS to confirm the validity of and enhance the information provided in the tips. These queries do not occur in ICE-CETS itself nor is there a system-to-system connection between ICE-CETS and these other data sources. Any relevant results are entered into the appropriate ICE-CETS record by the CES personnel, and will be used in generating any investigative referral to the field, if any. ICE-CETS also uses publicly available online services to conduct an IP lookup so that the appropriate entity can be identified and served with a subpoena. ICE-CETS will submit IP addresses to the IP lookup service and will receive the registered owner of the IP addresses from the service.

In instances where an email address or a subscriber online ID is provided as tip information, a subpoena can be sent to the identifying company or entity that is identified in the email address (such as POPULAR would be contacted for tonytone@popular.com). If it is unclear which company or entity owns the address or ID, CES personnel can search for the domain registered in the email address using a publically available information database.

2.4   Privacy Impact Analysis: Describe any types of controls that may be in place to ensure that information is handled in accordance with the above described uses.

ICE-CETS access will be limited to authorized CES personnel (special agents, criminal research specialists and officers) conducting official criminal child exploitation enforcement and investigative activities. As described in Section 8 of this PIA, security and access controls are in place to mitigate the risk of unauthorized individuals gaining access to information in the system. Users take mandatory annual privacy and security training, which stresses the importance of authorized use of personal data in government systems. Individuals who are found to access or use ICE-CETS data in an unauthorized manner will be disciplined in accordance with ICE policy, and may be subject to criminal sanctions for misuse of Federal information systems. These and other controls described in this PIA ensure the system is used only by authorized users for the intended purpose.

Due to the sensitive nature of ICE-CETS tips, access to the system is limited to authorized CES personnel conducting child exploitation investigations. Also, due to the investigative nature of child exploitation crimes, information in ICE-CETS will only be shared with other law enforcement personnel that are authorized to conduct child exploitation investigations.

Section 3.0 Retention

The following questions are intended to outline how long information will be retained after the initial collection.

3.1 What information is retained?

ICE-CETS retains tips involving suspected violations of child exploitation statutes, information returned to ICE from served subpoenas, and investigative research conducted by CES personnel. Subpoenas, and copies of subpoenas, are not stored within ICE-CETS.

3.2 How long is information retained?

ICE-CETS records are retained for 75 years. The records are deleted only after verification that they are not part of any legal hold and no longer needed for business purposes. The 75-year retention period is necessary due to recent changes to the statute of limitations for the prosecution of persons who have committed crimes involving child exploitation. Because of these changes, the tips maintained in ICE-CETS remain useful to law enforcement for the lifetime of the offenders because charges can now be filed regardless of the length of time since the crime occurred. Due to the high recidivism rate for the this type of crime in particular, and the fact that pedophiles are known to continue to be offenders even in their later years, the maintenance of this data may also be invaluable in identifying such offenders in future cases. The offender may follow the same or similar modus operandi, which ICE-CETS may be able to assist in identifying. Having the historical data available is vital to quickly identifying any new child exploitation crimes committed by such an offender.

Copies of subpoenas and the information returned are retained in the investigative case file and retained for the duration of the retention period for that case file in accordance with ICE investigative records retention requirements. If the subpoena and subpoenaed information are not part of an investigation, those records are retained in accordance with ICE investigative records retention requirements.

3.3 Has the retention schedule been approved by the component records officer and the National Archives and Records Administration (NARA)?

ICE is currently establishing a records retention schedule for ICE-CETS records.

3.4 Privacy Impact Analysis: Please discuss the risks associated with the length of time data is retained and how those risks are mitigated.

Privacy Risk: ICE-CETS retains data for a significant period of time, increasing the risk that the data will be misused, corrupted, or inappropriately disclosed.

Mitigation: Data in ICE-CETS is retained for 75 years for law enforcement purposes to provide historical information regarding individuals or enterprises that are known or suspected to have violated these criminal laws. The overwhelming majority of the tips in ICE-CETS are received from other law enforcement agencies that obtained the information based on reasonable suspicion or probable cause that a violation had taken place. Although ICE may not immediately forward the tip to a field office for additional investigation in cases where the offender cannot be identified, lack of identification does not negate the fact that a violation has occurred. Therefore, the data needs to be retained for an extended period so it is available for consideration as an additional part of the puzzle that will eventually identify the violator. In addition, access to ICE-CETS data is limited to CES personnel with a current need to know. Additionally, ICE-CETS management will conduct user audits annually to ensure records are accessed with appropriate need-to-know.

Privacy Risk: ICE-CETS may retain public tip data that was made maliciously about an individual who has not engaged in any actual wrongdoing.

Mitigation: If any tips received from the public are found to be false, the tip will be annotated as such in the system and retained to document that the tip was investigated and found to be false. Such tips will also be retained to ensure that false tips made by the same source in the future are identified so appropriate action can be taken if the source is believed to be acting maliciously.

Section 4.0 Internal Sharing and Disclosure

The following questions are intended to define the scope of sharing within the Department of Homeland Security.

4.1 With which internal organization(s) is the information shared, what information is shared and for what purpose?

ICE-CETS information is not shared with other components of DHS.

4.2 How is the information transmitted or disclosed?

ICE-CETS information is not transmitted or disclosed to other components of DHS.

4.3 <u>Privacy Impact Analysis</u>: Considering the extent of internal information sharing, discuss the privacy risks associated with the sharing and how they were mitigated.

ICE does not share ICE-CETS information with other DHS components.

Section 5.0 External Sharing and Disclosure

The following questions are intended to define the content, scope, and authority for information sharing external to DHS which includes Federal, state and local government, and the private sector.

5.1 With which external organization(s) is the information shared, what information is shared, and for what purpose?

ICE discloses IP addresses associated with tips to automated IP lookup services to help identify the correct owner of the IP for subpoena process. When conducting these IP lookups, the lookup service does not receive information about who is requesting the lookup or the purpose. When a subpoena is issued to another entity such as a corporation or an ISP, ICE only discloses the minimal information necessary to obtain the desired information in return (online ID, email address, user name). As a general rule, ICE only discloses minimal information to entities necessary for them to perform their legal obligations as defined in the subpoena. The subpoena does not include a description of the alleged criminal activity.

ICE discloses tips on an as needed basis to the appropriate federal, state, local, tribal, foreign, or international law enforcement agency in order to facilitate their investigation of child exploitation crimes within their jurisdiction. ICE may send the original tip data, such as a list of seized IP addresses, or it may send a more formal investigative referral – similar to the referrals it sends to ICE field offices, which include both the original tip information and information gleaned from the subpoena process. All information shared is in accordance with governing law and policy.

5.2 Is the sharing of personally identifiable information outside the Department compatible with the original collection? If so, is it covered by an appropriate routine use in a SORN? If so, please describe. If not, please describe under what legal mechanism the program or system is allowed to share the personally identifiable information outside of DHS.

ICE-CETS information is covered by the External Investigations SORN (DHS/ICE-009, December 11, 2008, 73 FR 75452). Sharing of this information with other law enforcement agencies and with entities for purposes of subpoenaing additional information is covered by existing routine uses in the SORN.

5.3 How is the information shared outside the Department and what security measures safeguard its transmission?

Information will be shared from ICE-CETS via emails and email attachments and digital media such as CDs to appropriate federal, state, local, tribal, foreign, or international law enforcement agencies in order to facilitate their investigation of child exploitation crimes within their jurisdiction. In some cases, paper printouts of tips or the results of queries against the ICE-CETS database may also be shared. In cases involving sensitive information password protected files, encrypted email, or secure couriers will be utilized.

Subpoenas are served via email, fax, or paid courier/shipping service, depending on the preference of the entity.

5.4 Privacy Impact Analysis: Given the external sharing, explain the privacy risks identified and describe how they were mitigated.

Privacy Risk: Due to the broad national and international nature of the threat of child exploitation, ICE must share information to combat these crimes effectively, which may increase the chance of misuse and inappropriate disclosure.

Mitigation: Federal, domestic and international law enforcement agencies adhere to strict internal policies when handling sensitive material, such as information related to child exploitation.

Privacy Risk: ICE may need to disclose limited information to an entity via a subpoena to identify potential offenders and gather evidence to prosecute crimes, which may reveal personal information about an entity's clients to the entity.

Mitigation: Subpoenas sent to entities only include the information necessary for the entity to successfully execute its obligations under the terms of the subpoena. The subpoena does not include a description of the alleged criminal activity.

Privacy Risk: The IP lookup services used to identify the appropriate entity on which a subpoena may be served may use the queries it receives inappropriately.

Mitigation: Generally, the IP lookup services only provide a geographic location when it receives a query regarding a particular IP address. In some cases, they may also provide contact information for a specific company. It is unlikely that they will attempt to determine which queries come from government offices. Further, it would be extremely difficult for them to determine which particular component of DHS or the Federal government is querying their database and for what purpose.

Section 6.0 Notice

The following questions are directed at notice to the individual of the scope of information collected, the right to consent to uses of said information, and the right to decline to provide information.

6.1 Was notice provided to the individual prior to collection of information?

In most cases, because of the DHS law enforcement purposes for which the information is collected, opportunities for the individual to be notified of the collection of information may be limited or nonexistent.

6.2 Do individuals have the opportunity and/or right to decline to provide information?

In most cases, because of the DHS law enforcement purposes for which the information is collected, opportunities for the individual to decline to provide information may be limited or nonexistent.

6.3 Do individuals have the right to consent to particular uses of the information? If so, how does the individual exercise the right?

In most cases, because of the DHS law enforcement purposes for which the information is collected, opportunities for the individual to consent to the particular uses of information may be limited or nonexistent.

6.4 <u>Privacy Impact Analysis</u>: Describe how notice is provided to individuals, and how the risks associated with individuals being unaware of the collection are mitigated.

Privacy Risk: Opportunities for notice may be limited or non-existent.

Mitigation: The publication of this PIA gives the public notice that ICE collects and analyzes tips to combat child exploitation.

Section 7.0 Access, Redress and Correction

The following questions are directed at an individual's ability to ensure the accuracy of the information collected about them.

7.1 What are the procedures that allow individuals to gain access to their information?

Individuals may request access to records about them in ICE-CETS by following the procedures outlined in the External Investigations SORN (DHS/ICE-009, December 11, 2008, 73 FR 75452). All or some of the requested information may be exempt from access pursuant to the Privacy Act in order to prevent harm to law enforcement investigations or interests. Providing individual access to records contained in ICE-CETS could inform the subject of an actual or potential criminal, civil, or regulatory violation investigation or reveal investigative interest on the part of DHS or another agency. Access to the records could also permit the individual who is the subject of a record to impede the investigation, to tamper with witnesses or evidence, and to avoid detection or apprehension.

In addition to the procedures above, individuals seeking notification of and access to any record contained in this system of records, or seeking to contest its content, may submit a request in writing to:

ICE FOIA Officer

800 North Capitol Street, N.W.
5th Floor, Suite 585
Washington, D.C. 20528

Individuals may also submit requests by fax at 202-732-0310 or by email at ice-foia@dhs.gov. Please see the ICE FOIA Office's website for additional information (http://www.ice.gov/foia/index.htm). If an individual believes more than one component maintains Privacy Act records concerning him or her the individual may submit the request to the Chief Privacy Officer, Department of Homeland Security, 245 Murray Drive, S.W., Building 410, STOP-0550, Washington, D.C. 20528.

7.2 What are the procedures for correcting inaccurate or erroneous information?

If individuals obtain access to the information in ICE-CETS pursuant to the procedures outlined in the External Investigations SORN (DHS/ICE-009, December 11, 2008, 73 FR 75452), they may seek correction of any incorrect information in the system by submitting a request to correct the data. The data correction procedures are also outlined in the External Investigations SORN. All or some of the requested information may be exempt from amendment pursuant to the Privacy Act in order to prevent harm to law enforcement investigations or interests. Amendment of the records could interfere with ongoing investigations and law enforcement activities and may impose an impossible administrative burden on investigative agencies.

In addition to the procedures above, individuals seeking notification of and access to any record contained in this system of records, or seeking to contest its content, may submit a request in writing to:

ICE FOIA Officer
800 North Capitol Street, N.W.
5th Floor, Suite 585
Washington, D.C. 20528

Individuals may also submit requests by fax at 202-732-0310 or by email at ice-foia@dhs.gov. Please see the ICE FOIA Office's website for additional information (http://www.ice.gov/foia/index.htm). If an individual believes more than one component maintains Privacy Act records concerning him or her the individual may submit the request to the Chief Privacy Officer, Department of Homeland Security, 245 Murray Drive, S.W., Building 410, STOP-0550, Washington, D.C. 20528.

7.3 How are individuals notified of the procedures for correcting their information?

The procedure for submitting a request to correct information is outlined in the External Investigations SORN (DHS/ICE-009, December 11, 2008, 73 FR 75452) and in this PIA in Questions 7.1 and 7.2.

7.4 If no formal redress is provided, what alternatives are available to the individual?

As stated, individuals may submit Privacy Act requests for information and correction, which will be reviewed and corrected on a case-by-case basis.

7.5 <u>Privacy Impact Analysis</u>: Please discuss the privacy risks associated with the redress available to individuals and how those risks are mitigated.

Privacy Risk: Opportunities for access and redress may be limited or non-existent.

Mitigation: Redress is available through requests made under the Privacy Act as described above; however, providing individual access and/or correction of the records may be limited for law enforcement reasons as expressly permitted by the Privacy Act. Permitting access to the records contained in ICE-CETS could inform the subject of an actual or potential criminal, civil, or regulatory violation investigation or reveal investigative interest on the part of DHS or another agency. Access to the records could also permit the individual who is the subject of a record to impede the investigation, to tamper with witnesses or evidence, and to avoid detection or apprehension. Amendment of the records could interfere with ongoing investigations and law enforcement activities and may impose an impossible administrative burden on investigative agencies.

Section 8.0 Technical Access and Security

The following questions are intended to describe technical safeguards and security measures.

8.1 What procedures are in place to determine which users may access the system and are they documented?

Direct access to ICE-CETS is strictly controlled by the program manager in cooperation with the system administrator. Direct access to ICE-CETS is limited to authorized CES personnel investigating violations of child exploitation statutes.

User access is controlled by the ICE-CETS administrators. The system restricts a user's data access rights depending on the level of permissions granted in accordance with the user's system profile. User access to ICE-CETS is in the following roles:

- "Investigator" roles have read-write access but cannot delete records.
- "Read only" roles have read-only access and cannot edit the records.
- "Manager" roles have full read-write access and may edit and delete records.

All ICE-CETS users have "Investigator" roles on records pertaining to their own cases. They have "read only" roles on all other cases on the system. Only the Child Exploitation Section Chief and ICE-CETS Program Manager have "manager" roles.

8.2 Will Department contractors have access to the system?

Yes. ICE contractors have access to the system for the purpose of providing information technology services related to system development, maintenance, and operations. All contractors have appropriate security and suitability clearances prior to being granted system access.

8.3 Describe what privacy training is provided to users either generally or specifically relevant to the program or system?

All ICE personnel and contractors complete annual mandatory privacy and security training and training on Securely Handling ICE Sensitive but Unclassified (SBU)/For Official Use Only (FOUO) Information. Also all ICE agents are provided with general training on the sensitivity and appropriate use when they join the agency. Personnel assigned to the Child Exploitation Section are trained in Cyber Investigations and Child Exploitation.

8.4 Has Certification & Accreditation been completed for the system or systems supporting the program?

The Certification and Accreditation process is in progress and is expected to be completed by December 2009.

8.5 What auditing measures and technical safeguards are in place to prevent misuse of data?

The ICE-CETS server is located on a secure network that exists at the ICE Cyber Crimes Center. This secure network is not connected to the DHS network. The network may be connected to the Internet to facilitate a direct connection to public IP lookup services.[6] In the event that the secure network is connected to the Internet, its connection will be controlled by a firewall that will not accept incoming connections and will not send or receive any traffic from any site except the IP lookup services.

The ICE-CETS server is located in a keypad-isolated room that can only be accessed by system administrators, program managers and IT officers. Access to the door is restricted by key card. Server access requires an ICE-CETS account that is managed by the system administrator and ICE-CETS Program Manager.

---

[6] ICE submits IP addresses to an IP lookup service. The IP lookup service tells ICE where the IP address is located and which entity owns it.

User passwords are required for access to the ICE-CETS application. The user profiles defined in Question 8.1 limit user access to the data. Direct access to ICE-CETS is strictly controlled by the program manager in cooperation with the system administrator.

All actions conducted on the system are logged and auditable. The system logs User ID, login time, login attempts, logoff time, failed login attempts, data records changed, and data records deleted. Periodic audits on system usage are conducted by the system administrator in coordination with the ICE-CETS program manager.

8.6 Privacy Impact Analysis: Given the sensitivity and scope of the information collected, as well as any information sharing conducted on the system, what privacy risks were identified and how do the security controls mitigate them?

Privacy Risk: Users with access to ICE-CETS may divulge, or misuse, information contained within ICE-CETS.

Mitigation: The security protections, training, auditing, and oversight of the ICE-CETS system serve to prevent misuse or disclosure of the PII incidentally captured by ICE-CETS.

Section 9.0 Technology

The following questions are directed at critically analyzing the selection process for any technologies utilized by the system, including system hardware, RFID, biometrics and other technology.

9.1 What type of project is the program or system?

ICE-CETS is a SharePoint application built on a robust SQL Server database with data analysis tools supporting the de-confliction and referral of tips received pertaining to child exploitation crimes.

9.2 What stage of development is the system in and what project development lifecycle was used?

ICE-CETS is currently being developed with a target deployment date of December 2009.

9.3 Does the project employ technology which may raise privacy concerns? If so please discuss their implementation.

No.

Responsible Officials

Lyn Rahilly
Privacy Officer
U.S. Immigration and Customs Enforcement
Department of Homeland Security

Approval Signature

Original signed copy on file with the DHS Privacy Office

Mary Ellen Callahan
Chief Privacy Officer
Department of Homeland Security